HOMAGE TO THE BLACK ARTS MOVEMENT: A HANDBOOK

Also by **JUDY JUANITA**

FICTION

Virgin Soul

NONFICTION

DeFacto Feminism: Essays Straight
Outta Oakland

In memory of
Dhameera Carlotta Simon Ahmad
whose life embodied the unsung
women of the movement
who gave body soul
intelligence youth
succor
unsparing

HOMAGE TO THE BLACK ARTS MOVEMENT: A HANDBOOK

JUDY JUANITA

EquiDistancePress

Homage to the Black Arts Movement: A Handbook

ISBN--10--0--9716352--2--6

EquiDistancePress 490 Lake Park Ave.

P.O. Box 16053 Oakland, CA 94610

whoknewyouknew@gmail.com

Acknowledgments: "The Black House" in Virgin Soul; "(not) forgotten man" in PoetryMonthly.com; "Life is a Carousel" in Eleven Eleven. "Five Comrades in The Black Panther Party, 1967--1970" in the Weeklings.com; and "Meeting LeRoi Jones" in Black History Bulletin. Vol. 80, no. 1. Thanks to the Rini Templeton Memorial Fund for the cover/interior artwork of Rini Templeton. Back cover photos by permission and from the personal collection of Elizabeth Sarfaty.

WHAT IS THE BLACK ARTS MOVEMENT?

"Both inherently and overtly political in content, the Black Arts movement was the only American literary movement to advance 'social engagement' as a sine qua non of its aesthetic. The movement broke from the immediate past of protest and petition (civil rights) literature and dashed forward toward an alternative that initially seemed unthinkable and unobtainable: Black Power."
Kalamu ya Salaam, *The Oxford Companion to African American Literature*. New York: Oxford UP, 1997.

"Black Art is the aesthetic and spiritual sister of the Black Power concept....the Black Arts Movement proposes a radical reordering of the Western cultural aesthetic.... the political values inherent in the Black Power concept are now finding concrete expression in the aesthetics of Afro--American dramatists, poets, choreographers, musicians, and novelists."
Larry Neal. "The Black Arts Movement." Drama Review, 12 (Summer 1968).

Words/terms for study:

Inherently
Sine qua non
Aesthetic
Black Power
Western cultural aesthetic

TABLE OF CONTENTS

Standing in front of the Black Student Union office at San Francisco State, l.-r, T.C. Williams (holding Muhammad Speaks), Judie Hart, Ron Bridgeforth and JoAnn Mitchell, ca. Spring, 1967.
Photo by and used with the permission of Jerry Varnado

Introduction
By Judy Juanita

This handbook joins four literary genres which scrutinize the seminal Black Arts Movement [BAM] of the 1960s and 70s, a new voice and visibility for poets, writers, intellectuals, performing and visual artists. I participated as it created venues, publications, productions, opened doors to academia, one of which I went through at SFSU.

My novel, *Virgin Soul* [Viking 2013], follows a young black student in the 1960s who joins the Black Panther Party. Excerpted here from *Virgin Soul,* "The Black House" follows this young woman as she discovers this exciting new tradition.

In the 60 minute play/film script, "Life is a Carousel," a black academic, Layla, on her way to a Black studies conference, meets the forgotten founder of Black Studies, Diahlo Green. They spar with airport reservation agents about his fare and meet at the convention where blatant disregard for him continues by a whole new generation. At issue is the relevancy of the Academy, Black Studies and the struggle. At each step of the way, the new, including LGBT professors, crushes the old.

The essay, "Five Comrades in The Black Panther Party, 1967--1970," looks back at my youthful participation in the most influential black revolutionary organization of the late 1960s and 1970s. The second essay, "Meeting LeRoi Jones," is the first encounter of student and mentor.

The poetry selection, "(not) forgotten man," is a sonnet about a seminal figure, Amiri Baraka, of the BAM.

short

story

THE BLACK HOUSE

Allwood and I -- black guy and black gal in a silver gray beetle crossing the San Francisco--Oakland Bay Bridge -- had to be the only two beings on earth headed for the Black House in the Fillmore rehearsing how to say *hello* and *how are you* in Arabic.

"As--salaam--a--laikum," Allwood said, for the umpteenth time, enunciating every syllable.

"Wa--alaikum--as--salaam," I said, trying unsuccessfully to stop myself from saying, "Wall, the lake um's a salami, brother sister baloney, and most high potentate."

Allwood shook his head.

"I'm sorry. I take it back." We entered the city, passing the San Francisco skyline, the offices full of yellow light and reflected dusk. Allwood sighed. The bridge swaying was behind us. We drove to the Fell St. exit and up the hill. We practiced; or I practiced and Allwood corrected me.

When we reached Divisadero St., I broke down. "They won't allow me in if I don't say this exactly right? Who is the boss of Salaam and Sa--laikam, anyway? It sounds like Abbott and Costello meeting up as sheiks on the street."

"Believe it or not," Allwood said, "You're going to like it." We finally parked at Hayes and Broderick. I looked around for a black Victorian.

"I don't see it. I don't see a black house."

"Geniece, it's not painted black." In Oakland, I was at ease. I came from a big clannish family, had gone to school from elementary through jr. college in Oakland, my solar system. San Francisco was another universe. Allwood directed me to a Victorian jammed between two other

Victorians, no different from the others except it was a light green between celery and vomit.

"As--salaam--a--laikum," I said to Allwood.

"Wa--alaikum--as--salaam," he rang the bell.

A black man with skin the color of a Hershey bar and teeth stunningly white stood before us. I was startled. Allwood said the Muslim greeting to him.

"Yeah, Brother Allwood," the man's voice had a tone so deep it rumbled. He took my coat away from me. I wanted to take from him. His tone. His confidence. His beautiful darkness. Something.

"Is this the sister's first time here?" he said to Allwood. I couldn't let him not talk to me.

"As--salaam--a--laikum," I said. His bushy eyebrows rose.

"I'm Geniece Hightower. I've never been here before." I extended my hand to him. He looked at it and laughed. More rumbling. Inside me.

"You niggahs from Oakland is quaint," he said. I heard the words "niggers from Oakland" in a way I had never heard anyone say them. Did he sing them? Did his voice go up an octave on "niggahs" and back down on "from Oakland?" His voice, whatever that was coming from his dark neck, was like a boat bobbing on an ocean. I couldn't take my eyes from him.

"This is our fortress against the wolf," he said, leading us up stairs.

"The wolf?" I felt a quivery knot in the pit of my stomach. Was I afraid or intrigued? He laughed so hard I thought I should stop asking questions.

"Everybody. The system, the world, the city." he stopped at the top of the stairs and leaned on the railing. "The garbage in the streets, the past, the present, maybe the future."

He raised his coal black eyebrows. "Street niggahs come up with a lot of existential rhetoric too."

"Bibo," Allwood addressed him.

"Your name is Bibo?" I asked. What a crazy sounding name.

"Wanna check my birth certificate?" I felt like I was bobbing alongside him.

"Bibo, what time does it start?" Allwood's voice grounded and jarred me. I had forgotten him.

"Speeches for the good brother Allwood right in there," the brother pointed to a closed door. Allwood squeezed my arm. I watched, wordless, as Allwood walked in and the door closed behind him. I heard a faint, high--pitched man's voice inside that was overpowered by the smell of this Bibo's body cologne, his personality, by his closeness.

"You belong in here, "Bibo said, steering me into a kitchen where a woman was stirring something that smelled like lamb and garlic in a pan. He disappeared down the hall. She was slight, with kumquat-smooth skin, an ankle--length skirt draped on her. Her back a graceful arch over the pan, her head wrapped in a purple silk scarf. She didn't see me and I didn't want her to turn and catch me staring at her. The smell of what she was cooking together with her appearance was enough. I was hearing the words Ali Baba and the Forty Thieves and *as--salaam--alaikum* in a jumble in my head. I felt if I saw her from the front she might spring snakes from the top of her head and twist over and grab me away from myself. No! I wanted to shout out at her. No! You can't have it. I turned and walked down the hall. I wanted to find my friend--boy. Where was Allwood who had gotten me into this? I had to go into one of these rooms. What if, my goodness, I walked in on somebody doing it? All the house parties had a bedroom upstairs where somebody dumb would happen on somebody not so dumb. But this wasn't a house party. This was different. I took a deep breath and opened a door that had a poster of Malcolm X on it. Maybe Allwood would be in here.

The room had once been a good--sized bedroom but now there were four rows of wooden folding chairs, set up with an aisle about a foot wide. A speaker stood at a podium, two chairs on each side of him.

"Some people think this is paradise. California: we're free. The South is behind us. Jim Crow is behind us. The ocean is our frontier now. We're a part of the wild, Wild West ... Don't believe it." The speaker's voice was high--pitched and familiar.

But the room was lopsided because everybody in there was sitting on one side. I wondered whom the other side was reserved for. The men in each chair looked alike, unsmiling with big Afros and creamy brown skin. Did all of these people have clear complexions? Then I realized, as I was escorted with a very gentle but firm hand to the empty side, that the room was full of men. My heart picked up a beat and I became aware of my body, my legs, and my jeans that were tight and worn through, showing the inside of my thigh.

"You're not a part of paradise." the speaker said. Seated where I belonged, on the other side, all by myself, I recognized him from the black radicals outside of Oakland City College. "For you," he repeated, with the same rhetorical flourish he used on Grove Street in the middle of the afternoon. "California is paradise with rules, a paradise for fools. And the main rule for niggers, that is, the unschooled fools who still call themselves Negroes, the main rule is--"

He broke off and started laughing. He was tall, gangly, light complexioned, like the faded yellow of a man's shirt. In all those lunch times I had watched him with the Grove St. orators and taken leaflets for *Fair Play for Cuba* from him, I had never seen him look jive or relaxed. I thought that guys like him had taken a vow to be serious for all the coloreds who had gone before us and been made into hyenas by mean white people. But he was laughing a deep, hearty laugh. I could tell by his entire face and torso shaking that he was really laughing. How could he shake and bellow like that here in this foggy black heart of San Francisco and never have seemed at ease even once in the sunshine and touch--me--I'm blue skies of Oakland?

"Wait!" The word hit the room like a thunderclap. I started in my seat. I needed to go to the bathroom but even more urgently I needed to get his point. I was following him just like I'd followed the preacher's sermons on those interminable Sunday afternoons. Only then I would wait for the preacher whom Uncle Boy--Boy dismissed as ignorant to say something ungrammatical or simple and I could dismiss the whole sermon. But the Grove St. orators were different. They were book smart.

"That's what the man insists that you do. Wait for justice. Wait for equality. Wait until he gets ready to give you freedom. To give you justice. To hand out equality on a silver platter." The men started clapping. I clapped along with them. They stopped. I put my hands back on my lap.

He cleared his throat like a reverend and went on. I wondered if God awakened him in the middle of the night telling him what the next day's sermon should be. Only his God would be Malcolm X or Marcus Garvey. His God was definitely a black man who wore owly glasses and Big Ben Davis coveralls and carried a briefcase, like he did. And his God then probably was light skinned. All the guys sitting in this room were shades between sand and the shore. Maybe dark me was in the wrong room or maybe that was why I had to sit over here.

"--and then he concocts a rationale for why you have to wait. Not why you should wait, why you gonna wait. Dig it. He gets some Irish cracker -- who's probably been to Harlem twice in his whole life -- to put together a report and put his name on it. Yeah, the Moynihan Report--"

This sounded like Allwood's turf.

"Yeah, the Moynihan Report which just means some potato farmer's great grandson is getting over on you, making his name, his rep, paying for his wife to hire your mama to make her dinner and wash her underwear out by hand -- yeah, your mother, we know why sistahs' hands be so rough -- and sending his kids to a college you couldn't get in if you had straight A's and perfect SATs. I know because I was one of the first Negroes at Harvard. Went in a Negro, invisible and all that shit, came out a black man. Had to. It was either break through to my blackness or die. And you see me standing here."

The men clapped in unison. When I clapped, I broke the oneness.

"Yeah. Moynihan...the very name makes me want to take somebody out. Moynihan says 'the Negro Community' has been forced into a matriarchal structure which, because it's so out of line with the rest of American society ---- Dig that, you--outta--line Negroes, get back in line ---- he says we 'seriously retard the progress of the group as a whole.'"

I still needed to pee. The walls were lettuce green semi--gloss; somebody had done a nice job on the trim and the windowsills...almost--alabaster. Nice. And I still wanted to find Allwood. But the speaker was up to the clincher here in this bedroom auditorium.

"I don't know bout you but I got a daddy. Fo your ass," he said. "This lame ass white man is your Uncle Sam. And the same mothers and fathers he's disparaging -- which is a fancy, white man's way of saying 'putting your ass down,' yeah -- those same black people are paying his salary, slaving, paying taxes so the man can write this bullshit, get a Ph.D. off it, and keep you down where you can't even get up and fight cuz you busy trying to prove to him that what he's saying ain't so which he knows already and that's why he puts it out there. So you'll spend the next twenty--five years trying so hard to disprove a lie that it begins to sound like the truth and Moynihan, some potato farmer's great grandson, begins to sound like a prophet."

He was through. I had attended enough church to know that. The men began clapping.

"We don't need no handclapping."

They stopped. "And we don't need no more Jesuses. One was enough to keep us under the yoke for 400 years." Well, I didn't see a collection plate so I got up and slithered out so I wouldn't have to shake hands with the right reverend. But he caught up with me at the door.

"Sistuh," he said. Why did I nod?

"Is this your first time at the Black House?" Could he tell? Wasn't my complexion as clear as everyone else's?

"Don't be embarrassed," he said. Oh, shit, he could read my mind too.

"You're not dressed the way the sisters dress here." He pointed me with his hand on my elbow back to the kitchen. "Fatimah will give you the word. She's a Nubian sister. Queens speak a language only other queens can understand. Dig?"

"Nubian?" I asked.

"Yeah. New Being. Nu--bi--an. That's the word here."

He meant to direct me to the kitchen and I do know about manners but the other side of the house called to me. I heard drums, vibrations, thumping, somebody blowing poetry like a saxophonist was inside his throat. I followed the sounds to a second part of the Black House, another house connected by a passageway. I bobbed along, dealing with a ferocious conga beat. That was when I saw dancers. The first thing I noticed was dark, dark sisters, their hair trimmed and moving with their bodies like fitted caps. It was a dark world and I fit, or so I thought until I looked in the mirror where I saw rolling, twisting torsos around me like serpents. I looked like a Tarzan native on a Hollywood movie set. I looked wild and untamed, countrified. The dancers had sculptured Afros; I had hair all over the place. The dancers had African print draped around them; I had on jeans. It made me think of my family, the side where light people, the high--yellow side, just had to be light. That's all, be light and that's all. The women who were light didn't even have to know how to dance, just be light, which made them pretty. I knew the browner people in the family could be smart as hell, it was never enough. If you were brown, you better know how to do something and do it well. Even then, you didn't get slack. My cousin Clovese had her picture in her paper at work. I could tell she was real proud of it because she showed it around. But I heard my aunt say, "So dark you can hardly see her."

Fatimah stood in the kitchen as if she had been waiting for me all night. I touched my hair instinctively. In front of her, it felt wiry and woolly. She smiled, her face relaxing as if a sentinel had left.

"You are a queen. Beautiful," she said. I didn't know what to say. I had been called cute but dark, sexy but dark, even fine and dark. Not beautiful.

"You've never been called that, have you? A queen?" she asked, her voice soft and rich.

"Never," I said. *Napoleon nose* had been one of my nicknames from the cousins. I knew I had a small waist and pretty feet, my one physically perfect part stuck at the end of my scarred legs. Men had singled out parts, as if the whole me was worth very little but the parts, singly and in pairs, could be worth something at auction. I never believed men who said I was fine because I thought they used the word interchangeably with the thought of wanting to fuck me. The brother who had called her a Nubian woman came to the doorway of the kitchen.

"Tightening her up, huh?" he said.

"Harris," Fatimah's large brown eyes seemed to pour the word out to him. There was something soft and gentle in her tone, the way she said his name. I wondered if she had been cooking for him.

He turned and began talking at someone down the hall. "Let the white kids lead a palace revolt. Let the white man be divided. Divided he falls, united we stand. When the man closes ranks is when we should be alarmed. That's when he's at his deadliest."

He turned back to me and said to Fatimah, "Lumumba, Patrice Lumumba. She's got that same steady look in her eyes. She's got a chilling thing going down in her eyes. Yeah."

My only frame of reference for the word Lumumba was a very dark, dark--as--night boy in high school, with very African features. He was from the South. He wore Big Ben overalls and clunky workingman's shoes and the other kids called him Lumumba. He had a crush on me and my friends had made fun of me because of the way he followed me around. They had called me Lumumba's wife, which I had hated.

When Harris walked away, I felt free to ask Fatimah. "Am I seeing things wrong here or do I just happen to see mostly light--skinned brothers here with darker--skinned sisters?"

She laughed a tinkly crystal laugh. She was so feminine. I wondered what her hair was like under her scarf.

"You picked up on that, huh? These brothers have an elevated consciousness and, yes, they're trying to prove something. Allwood is your man, right?"

"He's my friend." Her long, tapered fingers waved like wands at my words.

"Harris, Allwood, our men, our light--skinned men in the movement, they feel deeply about us as sisters, as beautiful black women."

"Isn't that overcompensation?" I asked.

"Maybe you could see it as that. They want, most people want a mirror. When you look outwardly, unless you look in a mirror, you can't see yourself. You can't see if you're skinny or fat or white or black. You see the people around you. Whatever they are, that's what you feel you are. When you wake up in the morning, you wake up human, no age, no color, and no sex until your eye hits either a mirror or another person. Then it's instant. That's who you are -- who you sleep with, who you eat with. So I think these brothers have grown to resent being categorized, put down because of their light skin. They're trying to prove who they are inside so they won't be judged by the outside."

I felt a sense of alarm. "Then will they dump the dark--skinned sister once they've made their point?"

She laughed again. "Did Malcolm leave Betty?"

"Malcolm X's wife was dark--skinned?" I asked.

She got a book from a stack on the table and showed me their picture. "Brother Malcolm's overcompensation benefited us all. He became as powerful as we are. He exposed us to our power and that was his power. That's why they had to kill him."

She put the book back and walked behind me. "Let me show you something." With one deft movement of her hands, she twisted my hair, tighter than I had ever twisted it, into a ponytail. She pulled me up and we went to the mirror in the hall. I looked at her hands, at her long smooth fingers, with their white half--moons. They told me my mother had strong fingers with beautiful half--moons.

"Do you see how different you look with your hair off your face?" she asked. For so long, I had used my hair as my shield. To see myself in front of her as I saw myself in the morning was a shock.

"You are a beautiful woman," she said, turning my chin from side to side. "Look at your face, your jaw, those beautiful planes of Africanness. Look at the light picking them out. You're a thousand years old. They couldn't beat the African out of you. They couldn't fuck it out."

She wouldn't let go of my head. One hand held my hair tight from my scalp, and her other hand, satin cool, cupped my chin. "You have to say it," she said.

"Say what?"

"I am such a beautiful woman."

I said it.

"No. Looking at yourself, not me," she said. I said it again slowly, but it was hard not to look at her. She was beautiful.

"You are the one that no one can make unbeautiful. Say it as if it meant all the gold in creation was inside your beauty. Inside you."

I looked at myself in that mirror with her behind me and I saw what she saw. I wasn't only parts put together. I was a whole. She let go of my hair and it went back all over the place. It didn't matter though. I was not just my hair, or my pretty feet that no one ever saw first, or any other part of my body, not even my mind. I was whole and new and she had showed me how to see that.

Bibo came sauntering down the hall. Fatimah watched me as we walked away. He wasn't so overpowering now. We went to another part of the house but he kept talking, pouring poetic shit in my ear.

"Elvis ripped off Big Momma Thornton...The hound dog...Jughead was an agent provocateur for the FBI...Millie the model had silicone implants but we didn't want to hear it...Yeah...True Romance tears stop where the real ones start...Ike was a colored man...Dinah Shore's a fugitive from the Negro race...Sammy Davis, Jr. got that empty eye socket from the mob...Little Lotta's fat comes from the diethylstilbestrol in all those hamburgers she stuffs down her fat white gut...Even if we heard it, it would have gone in one ear and out the other...Archie and Veronica freaked on her daddy's bed...You gotta use your imagination, otherwise you'll just be thinking some guy is peeing inside you...Richie Rich made his money from black sugar workers in rural Cuba...Louie Louie was a flasher...Nkrumah has led Ghana into the future fabulous." He walked toward Allwood who was waiting with his coat on. Allwood looked strange and new too.

"Are you ready?" he asked, one hand on the door.

When we got outside, the cold night air hit my face, right on the spots where Fatimah had held my chin. Allwood was looking down the street at the VW. He tucked his chin into his chest. I looked back at the Black House.

"Yeah, I'm finally ready," I said. "Baby, let's go."

The next day, I went to the barbershop and had all my hair cut into a natural.

Sleek, short, very African.

Questions for Discussion

1. What does Bibo mean by "fortress against the wolf"?
2. What is existential rhetoric in this context?
3. Why does the speaker at the Black House call California "a paradise for fools"?
4. How would you film this since so much of it is interior monologue?
5. Write a one-page treatment, and then try a 20-30 minute screenplay of it.
6. Some students may want to make an animated short film, others a graphic rendering or comic.

POEM

(not) forgotten man

whassup, amiri, quixotic nobody
on life's big hand. are you a little finger yet?
a historical new jersey atrocity
mimeographing *yugen* in a booklet?

your honeymoon with fame lasted decades
you and dick gregory like opposable thumbs
working it coast to coast (though poorly paid
save the acolytes feasting on your crumbs).

you were compact but never an everyman
you blasted the bridges between black and white
then witnessed the new century, the taliban,
afghanistan, not afraid to be tagged anti--semite.

for an instant you were the black oracle at delphi.
is that nostalgia or wisdom in your darkening eye?

Questions for Discussion

1. Who was Amiri Baraka? What was his contribution to the Black Arts Movement?
2. Quixotic comes from Don Quixote, a character in a novel by Miguel de Cervantes, first published in 1605. Why does the speaker in the poem call "amiri" quixotic?
3. Why does the poet use lower case?
4. Pull up a picture of a mimeo machine and images of the magazine *yugen* that Baraka edited and distributed from a mimeo machine. When did he publish it? Note the price.
5. What is the oracle at Delphi? Anti--Semite? An acolyte?

play

or

film script

Life is a Carousel

Characters

Layla, a black academic in her early 40s
Diahlo, an older black once--famous poet, and architect, in his 60s
[All minor parts can be double or triple cast]
Female Reservation Agent, black, in her 20s
Male Reservation Agent, gay, any race, in his 20s
Dr. Kwame Montague, black, male
Chiz, black, bi
Prof. Munyungo, black, male
Fernandra Long--Abramson, black female prof
Zion the Hip Hop Prof, black male
Dr. Prettyman, black male
THE LAST BROTHER, black professor, middle--aged
Blues Chanteuse, older than everyone else

Act One
Setting: an airport terminal
Time: Long past midnight

Act Two
Setting: Outside a convention center's main hall
Time: The next two days

Setting: an airport terminal
Time: Morning rush

[Layla, reservation in hand, and the female reservation agent are talking at the desk. Layla is dressed ghetto--fabulous—dreadlocks and doorknocker hoops, and bohemian—black from head to toe]

FEMALE RESERVATION AGENT

What was your point of origin again?

LAYLA

Chicago.

FEMALE RESERVATION AGENT

The black hole. You from there?

LAYLA

No. Indiana. Gary. Started in Chicago, going to Philly.

FEMALE RESERVATION AGENT

Everything disappears in Chicago. Baggage, reservations, elephants. It's criminal.

LAYLA

Geez. If my stuff got lost.

FEMALE RESERVATION AGENT

Rerouted.

LAYLA

What happens to everyone in my group?

FEMALE RESERVATION AGENT

What's the group?

LAYLA

25 participants from the university—they're all part of the Black Arts Millennium.

FEMALE RESERVATION AGENT
The black thang? Jazz, poetries, culture.

LAYLA
A four--day black thang.

FEMALE RESERVATION AGENT
Lemme stop being so chatty and see what I can do for the cause…Chicago to Burlington…too far…LaGuardia…you do not wanna get stuck in New York…whoops, here's something for nothing. I mean *nothing*. But your group have to do Baltimore…with a three--hour layover.

[Diahlo, a compact man with long, gray dreads, his bags dragging, walks into the reservation area, tired, irritated and not paying them any attention]

But that price gets attached sequentially to your entire group…I just saved your company----

LAYLA
The university.

FEMALE RESERVATION AGENT
$2,300!

LAYLA
Ooh, thank you so much.

FEMALE RESERVATION AGENT
For the cause. Now maybe waiting till dawn won't be so bad.

DIAHLO

[Layla has not seen Diahlo. She sits, stretches her legs, and
opens a magazine. Diahlo walks up to the agent, waits for the agent to recognize him; her head is down, he clears his throat.]

Whazzup?

FEMALE RESERVATION AGENT

[Barely looks up]

Sir, can I help you?

DIAHLO

[Talks to no one in particular since no one is looking at him, almost slams down his ticket]

As usual, the airline is juggin' with me.

FEMALE RESERVATION AGENT

Sir?

DIAHLO

Check this ticket from my travel agent. I need a much cheaper ticket and the refund directly. Done all the time.

FEMALE RESERVATION AGENT

Sir, this ticket is from an institution. That's where any refund returns.

DIAHLO

Look closer, my name's there too. Diahlo Green.

FEMALE RESERVATION AGENT
Mr. Green, I see your name. That's not the issue. The refund goes back the way it came.

DIAHLO
Don't give me doodang. Give me a refund.

FEMALE RESERVATION AGENT
Sir, I can't.

DIAHLO
If I was Robert Redford, you could.

FEMALE RESERVATION AGENT
Sir, perhaps you need to sit and rest.

DIAHLO
You don't know it, but I created your life, the climate for you to get this job.

FEMALE RESERVATION AGENT
Sir, excuse me, I'm doing my job.

[Layla steps up and speaks to the agent.]

LAYLA
Diahlo Green? <u>Self--Determination and Survival for People of Color and Conscience.</u>

[The agent shrugs her shoulders; Layla turns to Diahlo]

DIAHLO
[Not mollified at all]
No less than. No more than.

FEMALE RESERVATION AGENT
What was your point of origin again?

LAYLA
[To agent] Mr. Green is the keynote speaker for the conference.

FEMALE RESERVATION AGENT
But his ticket wasn't booked from your university, Dr. Huff.

LAYLA

[Pulls Diahlo aside]

The agent just gave me a deal. I have an extra ticket. Take it and get your refund through your department.

DIAHLO

[Loudly] Fuck the department.

LAYLA

[A look of consternation at his swearing; turns to agent]

I have a ticket for him. Can you refund his?

FEMALE RESERVATION AGENT
Let me look into it, Dr. Huff.

DIAHLO

I can't get the time of day from my department. Fuck that shit.

FEMALE RESERVATION AGENT
Sir, that kind of language is not appropriate.

DIAHLO

Fuck appropriate. I invented a whole new language. New shit!

FEMALE RESERVATION AGENT
Your language constitutes a threat. I will call security.

LAYLA

[Still trying to work the ticket]

Can you make an exception?

FEMALE RESERVATION AGENT
He's hustling the airline…and I'll tell you something. His name is on a list here. He's pulled this before.

DIAHLO
My name's on a thousand lists. And I'm proud of it.

LAYLA
Do you know who he is?

FEMALE RESERVATION AGENT
What difference does it make?

[Punches more numbers, scrutinizes them.] We have something here. I think you're in luck. Yes, yes, yes, I got it.

DIAHLO
Fucking petty bourgeoisie.

AGENT
Sir, I'm calling security.

LAYLA
[To Diahlo]

Put your ticket in your pocket.

[To agent]

Please add his name to my list. And thank you again.

[Slips her arm through Diahlo's and gently walks him away, looking back at the agent]

This brother changed the world.

[Agent punches at computer and puts up "Closed" sign, leaves. They sit down.]

DIAHLO

We finally meet, the one and only Dr. Huff.

LAYLA

Layla, please.

DIAHLO

And they call me Mister Tibbs. [They laugh] Diahlo to you. Thank you for interceding. Women. Finesse.

LAYLA

More like compromise. I read your autobiography.

DIAHLO

First or second one?

LAYLA

Both.

DIAHLO

[He starts to bristle.]

First one's out of print.

LAYLA

Got both online.

DIAHLO

Money I never see.

LAYLA

I didn't pay that much, if that's any consolation.

DIAHLO

How much?

LAYLA

[Hesitates] With shipping, six bucks.

DIAHLO

That's a crying shame.

LAYLA
I wanted to get to it before the symposium. You're such an important figure of the 20th century.

DIAHLO
This is the 21st century.

LAYLA
I know. I mean, I meant a seminal influence.

DIAHLO
Which you know all about third--hand? Learned it at your mother's knee? [She flinches] I studied the program. I see where there are two literary panels in the program, one hip--hop, and one slam poetry. You'd think being *seminal* and *such an important figure of the damn 20th century* would rate a panel.

LAYLA
You're keynoting. You set the whole tone.

DIAHLO
That's a load of crap. Niggahs won't even arrive till lunch, day two. You planned on a light turn out for the first night.

LAYLA
[Pissed] I'm changing clothes

[gathers her bags, walks toward ladies' room]

No fights if nobody's there. No death threats either. Nobody wants to go back to 1996. And the brouhaha at Seattle.

[As she walks away from him, he's still talking as if she can hear him. Dr. Prettyman arrives with carry--on.]

DIAHLO

Miz Layla, don't believe everything you read in the *Village Voice*. The writers who labeled our heated conversations as death threats also sell woof tickets. That's how people get reps when they don't have real talent.

[Dr. Prettyman and Layla practically collide as she exits and he enters]

DR. PRETTYMAN

Dr. Huff, pleased to finally meet you. Your pictures on Facebook don't do you justice.

LAYLA

Are you Thee Socialite Dr. Prettyman? What a name. Made up, right?

DR PRETTYMAN

Prettyman is the family name. If nothing else I come from a line of pretty men. My mother's side gave me intelligence.

DIAHLO

Sometimes folks make a big deal out of nothing because they know everything's already been done for them. It's called floorshowing.

DR PRETTYMAN

[Keeps walking briskly to catch his flight, stops at the door to the women's lavatory where Layla is entering, talks to her as if an afterthought hits.]

That was Diahlo Green? Man, he grayed. I'm surprised he's still coming out. Where the old guy's back--up singers?

[He laughs at his own joke and walks off. She goes in to change. Reservation agent returns, leaves the "CLOSED" sign up, works at computer and takes a call.]

FEMALE RESERVATION AGENT

Mr. Diahlo, good news. I can exchange your ticket for one of Dr. Huff's and give you the difference.

DIAHLO

[Gives the agent the ticket]

How much?

FEMALE RESERVATION AGENT

…$178!

DIAHLO

Bullshit! She <u>gave</u> me one of hers.

FEMALE RESERVATION AGENT

Excuse me.

DIAHLO

Do better.

FEMALE RESERVATION AGENT

You trying to get--over, I don't care how famous you were. Back in the day. You just a hustler to me.

DIAHLO

I want that measly $178 <u>and</u> my ticket refunded. Here and now.

[Agent hands him the ticket back with disgust. Layla comes back in African garb. Diahlo turns to look, his back to the counter.]

What's this? Your once--a--year Look--like--an--African Queen costume? It's wearing you like a cheap suit, Dr. Huff.

[The female reservation agent shakes head as she gathers bags and jacket, and leaves. The lights change because the sun is dawning. The airport ventilation starts humming. Chiz, the bisexual prof, walks in, eyeing ahead of him a male reservation agent with flamboyantly gay gestures, who comes in, conscious that he's being checked out by Chiz. When this new agent takes the sign down, and places himself firmly behind the counter, he puts on a facade of masculinity for the public. Layla unwraps the African robe; her street clothes are on underneath. Chiz checks it all out, shaking his head at the agent's actions.]

MALE RESERVATION AGENT

Looking good. Looking for love.

DIAHLO

Boho is always in fashion.

LAYLA

I didn't know I was so boho. And, no I'm not looking for love. I'm making a statement.

DIAHLO

You're rocking it.

[Diahlo walks over to the agent, midway remembering to pimp--walk.]

Say, man, can you work that technology so I can get on the flight with my lady here? Get this ticket, which is useless to me, refunded? And be gone.

MALE RESERVATION AGENT

[Punches a while] Looks like it.

DIAHLO

[Talks man--to--man] You can refund me this ticket now? The agent before you gave me endless bullshit.

MALE RESERVATION AGENT

[Punches more] Yeah. I can get you a refund, ah, right now, if you have ID.

CHIZ

Man, this is the incomparable Diahlo Green.

[Layla turns and sees him for the first time]

LAYLA
Chiz, you made it for the keynote. You're always on time. [They embrace]

CHIZ
I take care of biz.

DIAHLO
My man.

CHIZ
Not for much longer. I'm--

MALE RESERVATION AGENT
Chiz! Where you pick up that name? Too close to jizz if you ask me.

CHIZ
[flirting]
But I didn't ask you, now, did I?

MALE RESERVATION AGENT
[to Diahlo]
You are over 65?

DIAHLO
What's that got to do with it?

MALE RESERVATION AGENT
[Conspiratorially] I can get you senior rate – half your money back on the spot -- for a one--time family emergency on trips less than a thousand miles.

DIAHLO
Never heard of that.

MALE RESERVATION AGENT
And you get this special life insurance, 250 grand, for $155 cash upfront, right here. Only from me. [Lowers his voice] Got to hustle.

What I make is chump change. But you come out ahead. Don't worry.

[Layla comes back up, primping to face the new day. The men do the power handshake; the clerk is all smiles.

Diahlo catches his composure and makes a pretense of intimacy with Layla for the agent's sake.]

DIAHLO

Sweetness, my man needs your John Hancock.

LAYLA

Oh, good, you worked out the ticket thing. Make your department give you comp days. That's what we do. Get the equivalent. Then you can say fuck em.

[With a loud rumble the baggage carousel starts up, startling Diahlo, but not Layla who is getting her wallet from her bag. He sits down, whipped, and goes into his wallet for the cash, her back to him.

She walks, wallet in hand, with spring in her step to the reservation desk.

He holds the cash up for the agent to see. The agent nods to Diahlo.]

MALE RESERVATION AGENT

[Diahlo walks behind Layla. The agent is back in flamboyantly gay mode.]

Let me take care of this, girlfriend [hands her a new itinerary.] And boyfriend [snatches the cash from Diahlo in one swift move which Layla doesn't catch] I'll take care of you too. Mama got game for everybody [eyes Chiz].

CHIZ

So I see, mama.

[Layla and Diahlo load baggage. Walk onto ramp. Agent puts the CLOSED sign up, and he and Chiz get to talking and laughing.]

MALE RESERVATION AGENT

White people clothes. Black people clothes. Gay clothes. Straight clothes.

CHIZ

Trannie dress. Bi dress. If it feels good, it's all right.

SCENE TWO

[THE LAST BROTHER, a professor, walks in, luggage in hand.]

THE LAST BROTHER

Diahlo Green. Uh, Professor Dr. Diahlo Green. Have they knighted you yet?

DIAHLO

You the last brother I expected to be seeing. Abatagani.

THE LAST BROTHER

Abatagani, humph. Haven't seen you in a blue moon.

DIAHLO

Maybe you trying to avoid me, so you wouldn't have to pay me that $400 your black ass been owed me since the 20th century.

THE LAST BROTHER

I paid you that money, sent you an invoice from my college bursar.

DIAHLO

You ain't nothing but a Y2K Negro.

THE LAST BROTHER

I swear on my momma's grave.

DIAHLO

Don't jump bad with me. I known you since before you got published, before you got tenure at that piddling--ass junior college.

THE LAST BROTHER

You think I'm still meek and timid. You're mistaken.

DIAHLO

You owe me $400. And interest.

THE LAST BROTHER

As for giving you money twice, I'm onto that. You can't swindle me. Kiss my sweet black ass.

DIAHLO

Oh, you sweet now?

THE LAST BROTHER
Figure of speech. And we can take it outside. If that's what you want.

DIAHLO
Aw, I didn't mean anything. It's just so much back and forth now. Men not into women, women into women, men into men.

THE LAST BROTHER
It's been like that since forever. You gotta deal with your homophobia. I'm sorry for your loss. Your daughter didn't deserve to be murdered because she was a lesbian.

DIAHLO
She wasn't killed because of homophobia.

THE LAST BROTHER
Yes, she was. He killed your youngest child.

DIAHLO
Negro was crazy.

THE LAST BROTHER
One thing Marx said is to never allow the proletariat into the central committees because they're too close to the police.

DIAHLO
He wasn't political. Just a crazy Negro.

THE LAST BROTHER
Marx was referring to criminals and informants. And the central committee includes your family. You allowed your older daughter to marry

him, a brother who served time for dealing drugs. That makes him a criminal. And criminals are not to be glorified.

DIAHLO

How many times have I gone to jail? Man, we are all criminals in the man's eyes.

THE LAST BROTHER

But we are not all criminals in our own eyes. You even wrote that when you first got to know him, your family was playing charades, and he stumped everyone.

DIAHLO

The word was *criminal*, and he kept pointing to himself. We couldn't figure it out. He just laughed and--

THE LAST BROTHER

He said it, loud and clear, that night. "I am a criminal." And you brought him into your family. That's why he had the mind set to kill your daughter and her partner who had not a damn thing to do with his life problems.

DIAHLO

So, wise one, what would you have done in hindsight?

THE LAST BROTHER

[Sets down his bags]

I will fight tooth and nail against any of my daughters bringing a thug into my family, unless he proves himself a changed man. I believe in giving everyone at least one chance. If the person, or persons, fails, out, they go, especially if they have a propensity for violence.

DIAHLO

Every oppressed person has a propensity for violence.

THE LAST BROTHER

If Marx and Mao recognized "hooligans" for what they are, then Marxist--Leninist Diahlo Green should have been able to as well. The lumpen proletariat talks a good game, but follow--through's a different story.

DIAHLO

Yet here we are in this terminal and you threatening to kick my ass. You talking shit.

THE LAST BROTHER

My issue is that I am not to be fucked with by anyone, especially when it's a ploy to get over on me. At my community college – they dropped the *junior* decades ago, Diahlo – I work in a toxic, hostile and racist environment that's caused me physical and mental health issues. I'm on medical leave and in a Black Men's anger management group.

DIAHLO

What happened?

THE LAST BROTHER

I went south on a new colleague, who was running around telling students that I was an idiot and not to take my classes. The students stood up for me and informed the dean who did nothing. When I confronted this colleague, he shoved me in the face and I kicked his white monkey ass.

DIAHLO

So it wasn't thug violence. It was self--defense.

THE LAST BROTHER

I had to go to court for assault and battery, which was thrown out of court.

DIAHLO

Congrats.

THE LAST BROTHER

[Picking up his bags]

My flight's ready. My anger group's been good for me.

DIAHLO

More brothers could do with something like that.

THE LAST BROTHER

Whoever messes with any of us best bring lunch cuz it's gonna be a long day. Or night.

DIAHLO

Come to think of it, your college did send me some money. Maybe not $400 though.

THE LAST BROTHER

I'd check your receipts, Brother Green. You, of all people, should know that character assassination is as lethal as any weapon that pierces flesh. I have not turned my back on the struggle. My issue with you has nothing to do with your tragedy. *Akubariki*.

DIAHLO

Bless your damn self.

[Last Professor shakes his head and walks off.]

I don't need a damn blessing.

[The carousel begins to turn. Diahlo goes into a snore. The carousel stops abruptly. Diahlo wakes, starts counting his money again.]

Act Two
SCENE ONE

[Outside the convention hall in a large foyer. Next door to the convention is a bar/lounge where the fabled Blues Chanteuse sings, plays piano, makes notes, looks at the parade of professors walk past her. Throughout the conference, each stops to listen to her momentarily, puts paper money in the jar and walks on by. A cardboard life--size Obama stands in place in the foyer, and another on the dais. The large sign next to the one in the foyer has the titles of conference presentations in block letters. People walking through the foyer take their picture with the Obama figure. The introduction of Diahlo comes over the loudspeaker, suddenly loud. He's in the background, almost out of sight, on a mike system that fades in and out.]

ANNOUNCER [unseen]

My esteemed colleague from [inaudible] university--

DIAHLO

[Takes his glasses off]

Esteemed colleague!! What did they call Dick Gregory when they split his head open during the Watts riots? Mister Comedian. Mister Mark Twain, Mister Humorist? Unh unh…nigger. What did they call Skip Gates in Cambridge, Massachusetts, when he came home, from a trip to China no less, and his chauffeur gave him a hand with a jammed front door? Mister Public Intellectual? Professor Gates? Your President called it a teachable moment. I doubt that's what the Cambridge police called it.

[Puts his glasses back on]

We led the revolution. Not the so--called "metropolitan revolution of the sixties." That was urban planning gobbledygook for white flight from the cities. That's why I had to leave architecture and pioneer the black studies revolution. We were not AT the forefront. We WERE the forefront.

[Two young Profs with briefcases/man--purses step up to take selfies with Obama]

DR. KWAME MONTAGUE

This is the trope of the day. Diahlo Green is yesterday's trope.

CHIZ

Yesteryear.

DR. KWAME MONTAGUE

Yester century.

CHIZ

Antediluvian. Selfie here. Selfie there [points to Diahlo] Which would go viral?

DR. KWAME MONTAGUE

Just get the man--purse, honey--pie.

LAYLA

[Strides up in a new outfit, preens. The Profs slap hands]

Neither, gentlemen. Put this in your portfolio. [Repositions herself near the block lettered sign] The sign, the sign, brothers. Get me *and* the sign And put it on Instagram.

DR. KWAME MONTAGUE

Only if it includes my workshop, [positions himself] Public Housing, Urban Renewal and the Working Class.

DIAHLO

[The Profs and Layla take selfies as his voice gets miked forcefully. They walk off as he pontificates.] They needed us before and during the wars. World War I. World War II. The railroads, the ports, the factories. We made Chicago. St. Louis. Detroit. Newark. Philly, we left those beautiful magnolia trees with their strange fruit and came up north. Moved west. Los Angeles. Oakland. San Francisco.

[Two more Profs peruse the Obama figure, not impressed]

DR. KWAME MONTAGUE

Symbolism. Purely symbolic. Peek--a--boo progress. Feel good for five minutes.

CHIZ

Don't be so mean. He's got a heart. Knock--knock. [Knocks the figure. It buckles]

DR. KWAME MONTAGUE

As substantial as an In--and--Out burger. Couldn't stand up to the banks. But then again, being a black male in America is an emasculating proposition. I seem to remember that from adolescence. Bad memory, go away.

[They walk offstage, leaving the Obama tilted]

DIAHLO

When white folks left the city, what was ethnic became segregated. In Newark, the ethnic whites and Jews went to the Oranges. South Orange, West Orange, hah! Scotch Plains, Bergen County.

ZION THE HIP HOP PROF

By the way, I like this change. My seminar's title wasn't specific enough. She made it slick. "Every seminar is a collision," sayeth Miz Layla. Love that. Punch it up, baby. "The Collision between Hip Hop and Academia."

CHIZ

What was it before?

DR. KWAME MONTAGUE

"The Negative Repercussions of Academe on--"

CHIZ

Stop. I hate that word. Academe.

DR. KWAME MONTAGUE
Too Greek? Ak--uh--deem.
CHIZ
Spare me.
DR. KWAME MONTAGUE
Spare you? Don't forget. It's who we are. It's how we make our living. [They turn their attention to the podium where Diahlo speaks. Layla comes in another outfit]
DIAHLO
Then came the period between the big wars. Hah! Watch out. Whenever the man goes to war in the world--at--large, crosses those oceans, we get a break. But when he finishes overseas, he comes back to kickass. Our ass. So the federal government set up mortgages. Yes, folks, Uncle Sam subsidized the suburbs from 1930 to 1950. Before there was section 8 for Negroes, there was a Section 8 for white folk. They just called it FHA mortgages.
DR. KWAME MONTAGUE
I can't stand "the man."
CHIZ
Diahlo Green?
DR. KWAME MONTAGUE
No, of course not. The term – the man. So 20th century. My parents don't even use that term and they were Diahlo Green acolytes. They respected that he had mastered architecture and then established a new discipline, black studies.
DIAHLO
The man, the man, the man. Hah! He's still the man. He's still got the power that we don't understand that we possess. Six and ½ million of us migrated out of the ole Kentucky home, out of the Sip and sweet home Alabama. Following the North Star.

But the man, the man, was busy in containment mode.

DR. KWAME MONTAGUE

If he could just update his paradigm, I could process him.

LAYLA

That's our job, to process. Didn't we do that in grad school? Absorb, assimilate, release anew.

DR. KWAME MONTAGUE

Ad nauseam. That's why I can't do him. Rest it. I don't want to mess up my Lexus processing his shit.
[Layla shakes her head and turns her full attention to Diahlo]

DIAHLO

Did you know that 3/5ths – three of every five homes were financed by FHA? And only 2% of those FHA loans went to us folks.

DR. KWAME MONTAGUE

Okay. He's up to Gary Tobin and redlining. "Changing Patterns of Racial Segregation." 1987. C'mon, Diahlo Green, pull into the present, dude! You're still alive.

LAYLA

He doesn't need to do our job. He did his. He's an ancestor right now. Standing in front of us.

DIAHLO

Ferguson. It's the prime example of the man setting up segregation. Ferguson, damn fools! I'm coming down and speaking to you directly. Damn mike ain't working and nobody's here yet anyway.
[He grabs his speech and walks briskly with a limp to where they're standing]

CHIZ

[Head spins around]
Okay, old man!

DIAHLO

Ferguson. It's called the ghetto comes to the suburbs.

DR. KWAME MONTAGUE

Get on the case.

[Layla smiles and walks off]

BLUES CHANTEUSE

[Sings a few bars of "Come Rain or come shine"]

"I'm gonna love you like nobody's loved you, come rain or come shine. High as a mountain and deep as a river, come rain or come shine I guess when you met me it was just-

DIAHLO

When your people moved from St. Louis to Ferguson because they couldn't give their kids a decent education, the realtors steered them like cattle to Ferguson. White folks split St. Louis for greener pastures.

DR. KWAME MONTAGUE

They did the same thing all over the country. In Oakland, my cousins left Oakland, bought this big ass 5--bedroom houses in Antioch, not Brentwood or Walnut Creek.

DIAHLO

The real estate KKK. They don't wear white hoods. They promulgate white *neighbor*hoods.

DR. KWAME MONTAGUE

And they spend a hella lot of time and gas money back and forth to Oakland to visit the rest of us.

DIAHLO

Newark. Oakland. Sister cities.

ZION THE HIP HOP PROF

Hah!

DIAHLO

Different eras, same practice. Move em in, move em out.

DR. KWAME MONTAGUE

But only to the new ghettoes. Antioch is the new Oakland -- murders, robberies, assaults.

DIAHLO

Containment, containment. When you're an animal, you have to be kept with your own kind. Then you can be taken care of in a bulk lot.

[Layla comes back by. Chiz fingers her locks, picks off a piece of lint.]

CHIZ

Love your locks.

LAYLA

Love yours too.

CHIZ

Where do you get them done?

LAYLA

Not in Vermont. [They crack up] I fly home to Chicago to get my roots tightened. [Knocks Obama figure]. Home boy knows the deal. He had his barber from Chi town flown to DC at first.

CHIZ

I know, I know. At the press conferences, you could always tell when homeboy had somebody else cut it. Line all crooked cuz homeboy got one of those bigheads.

DIAHLO

Vermont. Humph. New Hampshire. Connecticut. Playgrounds of the public intellectuals.

LAYLA

More like Arkansas. Missouri. Nebraska. And Salt Lake City. Hardship posts. But I'm more at ease in Vermont than I ever thought I would be. I burrow in when it's winter.

CHIZ

[Blues chanteuse plays "cry me a river"]

If we were overseas in the State Department, we'd get hardship pay.

DIAHLO

But you wouldn't get tenure.

LAYLA

We get paid less to be isolated. When I visited my buddies in Cairo, they called it hardship pay. I tried to get to them the whole decade they were in Nairobi, but I was teaching summers, busy adjuncting at three colleges. By the time I finished my dissertation and became fulltime, my friends had left Kenya for Egypt. They left a thriving expat community for a hardship post.

[Expecting a response and getting only shrugged shoulders, she sighs and continues]

In grad school, Even crisscrossing those highways to get to part time gigs, I had people. Friends. My fellow students. When I graduated and got a position in the Midwest, I got called nigger from the back of those pickup trucks more times than I can count.

CHIZ

Maybe the Missouri Compromise is stuck in their throats.

LAYLA

My first winter in Vermont -- no name calling. just the cold, the snow, white people. I went to every conference I could. I started putting on small conferences myself. I can't exist in West Podunk on my guts alone. Not possible. Black people, brown people, juice, even if it spills and it's messy. I need it. That's why these conferences are so important.

DIAHLO

That so? Back in the day, they were fuckfests.

[Layla and the Profs laugh uncontrollably]

LAYLA

I guess the more things change, the more they stay the same.

CHIZ

Seriously, I know the work you put in to get this up and running. Thanks, girlfriend.

DIAHO

Who runs this crap?

LAYLA

Are you calling my conference crap?

DIAHLO

It's all crap. Don't fool yourself. [Goes back to his speech] Remember restrictive covenants? Those who forget their history gotta pete and repeat it. The US Supreme Court – the nano nano nine – upheld restrictive covenants. Uncle Sam is the King Landlord. King Slum Landlord.

[A coffee –cart comes by. The Profs and Layla go off after it. He realizes no one is listening.]

Coffee break? oppression is 24/7. But the bourgeoisie need lattés [yells at the universe]. Oakland? One of the five hippest places to visit – New Yawk Times 2014. Humph. don't get off the freeway on the wrong exit. "The man" destroyed West Oakland, moved out blacks for a post office and a free--way which crumbled anyway in the World Series earthquake. God is in the details. And the blues capital of the world…wiped out.

END SCENE

SCENE TWO

[Blues chanteuse starts counting the dollars in the jar. Diahlo walks out on his cane; the profs and Layla walk back in, lattes in hand. It's awkward as they maneuver in and out.]

LAYLA [giggling and gossipy]
I saw The Bad Ass Bards in Oakland.

CHIZ
Oh no you didn't. My dad used to book them in LA.

LAYLA
They bad ass all right...three hours late.

CHIZ
Three hours? Spare me.

LAYLA
Apologizing with some lame shit. Bad ass my foot. LameAss. And then had the nerve to say, "We got to eat first." And funk--asses pulled out a bag of fried chicken and started eating right in front of us. People giving side--eye all over the place. They're sitting on this couch like czars.

CHIZ
That's the thing with the brothers. They think the world revolves around them. No, you created a grand world. NEWSFLASH! It crumbled because you forgot that women are goddesses. We are supreme beings.

LAYLA
Wait. I thought you were a dude.

CHIZ
In another life, the one I left behind.

LAYLA
You're transgender?

CHIZ
I'm transgendering.

LAYLA
You mean you're transitioning.

CHIZ
I'm transgendering. Doing it my way. And we were goddesses before THEY were gods. [sings the lyrics]" It's a man's world, it's a man's world, but it

would be nothing without a woman or a girl." No, James Brown, James Brown, and James Brown, [with each repetition, points around] you died and that thinking died before you did.

LAYLA

Okay. Get this: while the fat--ass, I mean, bad ass bards were eating their grub, they decided they needed drink. The owner of the venue had his daughter serve their shaky shit asses. And the young woman got down on her knees and poured them tea, like an African geisha. I nearly gagged.

CHIZ

A complete misreading of African matriarchy. I wasn't put here to serve your sorry--asses. I didn't get a Ph.D. and read 300 books for my dissertation to serve some tubby--ass oh--gees. I don't think so.

[Blues chanteuse begins singing "Who Can I Turn To" for the next few beats, getting louder /softer]

LAYLA

[Pulls out her make--up kit]
I got to redo my makeup. Put my game face on,

CHIZ

Bye, Felicia. I need to do mines.
[They leave again, sharing makeup items]

DIAHLO

[He's been listening] Costumes. Go to your next get--up so you can fool some of the people some of the time, But not all of the people all the time.

END SCENE

[Blues chanteuse sings "Who Can I Turn To" louder /softer]

SCENE THREE

[Fernandra and Prof. Munyungo exchange and barter ivory and amber necklaces and bracelets. Blues chanteuse can be heard indistinctly.]

PROF. MUNYUNGO [pleased with jewelry]

Baby, you can drive my car.

FERNANDRA LONG--ABRAMSON

[She fingers his wedding ring.]

Not if it's in park.

(The Blues Chanteuse has a tip jar near one of the tables, marked "TIPS", she's tinkling the piano)

PROF. MUNYUNGO

That's an actual person singing. For the love of Christ, I thought that was recorded music hooked up to a bullhorn.

FERNANDRA LONG--ABRAMSON

(goes in wallet)

I better leave some moolah in her jar. She might put a spell on me otherwise.

(Pulls out money, leaves it with a flourish)

BLUES CHANTEUSE

It's a tip jar. Come sit down and give me a listen.

FERNANDRA LONG--ABRAMSON

Not today, but here--

(pulls out wallet to give more)

BLUES CHANTEUSE

Don't. This isn't about money.

MALE PROF

If it don't make money, it don't make sense.

FERNANDRA LONG--ABRAMSON

It you don't want more money, then why are you here? This looks like a venue to me.

BLUES CHANTEUSE

Have you heard of King Oliver? From the 1920s? Or Koko Taylor and Wang Dang doodle? That's not ancient history.

(They shake their heads)

There's a steady clientele for me here. Musicologists from the local colleges.

MALE PROF

We're part of the conference. Black Studies.

BLUES CHANTEUSE

That's odd, don't you think. I'm black, the blues are black, Bricktop was black, Estelle Yancey was black, Victoria Spivey was black, you're black, and I've traveled the world! Singing this purely American music, sung with Louis Armstrong when I was a girl, yet you've never heard of it. I'd say you were a bit beside yourself with privilege.

MALE PROF

I know Louis Armstrong played in brothels in New Orleans starting out. I'm an anthropologist, not a musicologist. I did spend three years in Kenya; they make a wonderful guttural sound when they end the young girl's passage to womanhood and then I was in Cameroon studying the Bamileke tribe.

BLUES CHANTEUSE

kossa kossa Like this? *mamako, mamasa, maka makossa*

[She sings from *Soul Makossa*, a popular 70s tune])

FERNANDRA LONG--ABRAMSON

The Massai tribe of Kenya? They perform clitoridectomy on the young girls. Then marry them off to old men. That's brutality. Torture. It's also rarely performed under hygienic conditions. Many of the girls are deformed and can't have children after that.

BLUES CHANTEUSE

I heard about genital mutilation when I toured the continent in the 1950s. It was right after independence. As a blues musician, I was introducing an important part of American culture. I was a cultural ambassador. It wasn't my place to change them.

FERNANDRA LONG--ABRAMSON

We have a seminar about to start.

BLUES CHANTEUSE

Don't let me hold you up.

FERNANDRA LONG--ABRAMSON

Please, let me contribute something.

BLUES CHANTEUSE

Come back at seven when I perform. Tips come after the act, not before.

END SCENE

SCENE FOUR

[Prof comes out, trying to drum up an audience]

ZION THE HIP HOP PROF

I have free DVDS. I'm featured with Digable Planets.

DIAHLO

Cornell did that already. Why are you still here?

ZION THE HIP HOP PROF

What do you mean by here? This conference?

DIAHLO

The universe, the galaxy. Here!

ZION THE HIP HOP PROF

This is my seminar. "The Collision between Hip Hop and Black Feminists in Academia."

DIAHLO

Whatchu trying to do? Rewrite the rulebook?

ZION THE HIP HOP PROF

They have a toehold in academia because of multiple entrees – Black Studies, Ethnic Studies, Women's Studies, Feminist Sociology, African Dance, Theology, English, Education, and Gender Studies. Shit, Librarian and Information Studies.

DIAHLO

Brother, we all came from different disciplines back in the day to form this new discipline, Black Studies. But I getchou. The Saint Mammy Syndrome. Black women are more acceptable. Us in trouble. Nigga man trouble.

ZION THE HIP HOP PROF

Say so. Say so.

DIAHLO

Let's not forget Black intellectuals are one of the most privileged populations around.

ZION THE HIP HOP PROF

Is there still a place called Black America?
[Lifts up Obama figure as if searching for him]

DIAHLO

Then again, they arrested Gates for B & E in his own home. Intellectual, my foot. Harvard, Yale, Princeton, be damned.

ZION THE HIP HOP PROF

[Holds up Obama] "C'mon, Beantown. Let's sit down over a beer. C'mon, copper, let's dialogue." [Sotto voce to the cardboard] POTUS, that was bullshit and you know it.

DIAHLO

Then again, they shouted bro down – "you a lie" – in his first State of the Union.

ZION THE HIP HOP PROF

He's supposed to be the supreme gangsta of the world. Prez!

DIAHLO

Nah. If you got to be the chair of your department--

ZION THE HIP HOP PROF

I am the chair.

DIAHLO

Okay, prez of the university, chancellor.

ZION THE HIP HOP PROF

I still wouldn't have control because?

DIAHLO

Puppets control puppets that control other puppets. [Two women, Layla and Chiz, get up and start reading poems]

CHIZ

"And the brother say, you so sexy, I bet the gods say your name when I come inside you."

DIAHLO

That's a damn shame. Taking Sonia Sanchez' poetry and turning it into gay porn. Somebody thought, "This a new genre of poetry, my pussy is delicious, my pussy tastes so sweet, my pussy, my pussy, it's like frankincense and myrrh" None of the poems gone say, my pussy stinks, it just plain stinks. Because that wouldn't fit coming out of a lady's mouth. Wouldn't be ladylike -- sweet and delicious-- and that's what the genre gets wrong. Sonia's point was the strength of the bond between the black male and black female, and strength ain't sweet. It's sweaty, funky and mixes up feminine and masculine, reconciling masculine and feminine, shadow with light. Funky sweat. Keep it funky, dahlings.

CHIZ

Funky sweet?

DIAHLO

Unh unh, funky sweat. Stuff that stinks. Stinks. stinks. Odoriferous, like fish heads.

CHIZ

Here y'go.

[Starts to recite "Street sonnet"; gets interrupted, ignored, reads louder, provocatively, fades away]

brothers get ferocious when they fuck
cuz bros got to represent when they fuck
they got to represent family, other black
men, your past lovers, the race, black history.
they bring all this into the bed so please
do not attempt to fuck a bro on a futon.
hollywood shows you how white men fuck
on tables and stairs and hard surfaces

marble staircases and walnut desktops. pullease!
to fuck a bro you need mattresses pillows
air bags sealyposturepedic waterbeds foam
and you best have a chiropractor in the next room.
bros work at fucking. they may say
fuck work but they work hard at fucking

DIAHLO

You can't have it both ways. Stand up for your bed sister and then bed the brother on the side. At some point, you're a traitor to both.

CHIZ

You telling me, stay in my own lane? It's called bi, bro. LGBTI.

ZION THE HIP HOP PROF

Playing both ends against the middle. One decade, the Black Nationalist mafia. Twenty years later, play the bush leagues, batting for the lesbian mafia to get tenure. When those tides change, you'll put your wet, middle finger in the wind to see which way it's blowing.

CHIZ

Jealous much?

ZION THE HIP HOP PROF

Truth leads. If you need to be Native American, you'll get a tribal affiliation and eschew Thanksgiving. I can see you putting a dot on your forehead and a sari on your sorry ass.

CHIZ

You are personally, literally and metaphorically an ass. I am Creek--Seminole and have the DNA test to prove it.

LAYLA

[Enters on that last exchange]
Let's turn down the room temp, people.

DIAHLO

Crabs in a barrel. All of you made tenure at the speed of lightning. And here I am adjuncting my way to retirement.

LAYLA

Guest lecturer, Berkeley. Diahlo Green, Duke University Archival Visiting Writer.

DIAHLO

Peanuts. Led nowhere.

LAYLA

NEA. Guggenheim.

DIAHLO

Fuck all y'all.

LAYLA

One grad seminar a year.

DIAHLO

My point exactly. That's not tenure.

LAYLA

You were writer--in--residence for nine years. That's travel year around.

DIAHLO

Yeah, out of sight, out of mind.
[Noise comes from the main room. Folks are partying to rap with R&B]
Fuck all y'all.
[Music blasts similar profanities]

END SCENE

SCENE FIVE

LAYLA

I been tryin to get over here and sit myself down with you.

BLUES CHANTEUSE

Yes, yes, I've watched you go by. Your attire is amazing.

LAYLA

Where you from?

BLUES CHANTEUSE

Camden, New Jersey.

LAYLA

I taught at Rutgers, Camden for a year. Camden, uh, ain't that where you gotta carry a .22 in your bootleg?

BLUES CHANTEUSE

My dear, are you under the mistaken impression that I can't speak proper English?

LAYLA

I'm sorry if I offended you.

BLUES CHANTEUSE

I'm multilingual. I've worn out seven or eight passports. Are you playing with a stereotype of blues artists being basically black hillbillies?

LAYLA

No, no, that would be the last thing I'd do. But I heard Ma Rainey in interview.
She wasn't the most educated person.

BLUES CHANTEUSE

Educated and ignorant aren't mutually exclusive...you know?
(Plays some keys on the piano, sings a scale)
Did you sing in Sunday School?

LAYLA

I'm atonal. Not quite tone deaf, but I did take dance lessons.

BLUES CHANTEUSE

What type? Don't tell me. Let me guess. Walk again.
[Layla walks]
Modern and tap. No ballet.

LAYLA

How can you tell?

BLUES CHANTEUSE

Your isolations. Training shows, especially when you walk.
(Plays a few bars of "Cast Your Fate to the Winds" by Vince Guaraldi)

LAYLA

I'm a patron of the arts now. I leave performing to the professionals.

BLUES CHANTEUSE

(Keeps playing)
How many years did you take lessons?

LAYLA

From the time I was eight years old until I left home for college.
(Starts some movement, lured by the music)

I loved to dance. It was a language. A foreign language that I used to express what English couldn't.

(Starts getting into it; Blues Chanteuse smiles, stops playing as she sees Layla is turned on by the act of performing. The Chanteuse starts playing an entirely different tempo and Layla adjusts)

BLUES CHANTEUSE

You're a natural dancer.

(They do a number of styles: ragtime, honky tonk, capoeira. They mesh, Layla losing herself in the styles rapturously until they go to a Nigerian melody and Layla's dancing seems to become tortured. She can do the elaborate extensions but looks pained. She stops. Then, the music stops. There is silence as Layla looks around.)

LAYLA

When I started learning African dance, I was a sophomore. I had to choose my major. It seemed so impractical. What was I going to do with a major in it?!

BLUES CHANTEUSE

Dance it. Teach it.

LAYLA

I couldn't. I lost my nerve. It was easier to decode the language of Shakespeare and the Bible--

BLUES CHANTEUSE

Than to express your own language.

LAYLA

At the time, it felt safer. Like I would be self--sufficient. I looked at other African dance students and I knew there wasn't enough work, jobs, dance troupes for all of us. I couldn't let myself go down that road. I didn't want to survive. I wanted to prosper.

BLUES CHANTEUSE

And you have.

LAYLA

I have.

BLUES CHANTEUSE

And how does it feel?

LAYLA

To be prosperous?

BLUES CHANTEUSE

Not to be able to use that other language.

LAYLA

I don’t have children. I didn't marry. I didn't follow that dream. I bite down on it sometimes, like when you bite your tongue. Not often, like now, when I see an authentic performance unexpectedly. As long as I schedule it and dress for it, I'm fine.

BLUES CHANTEUSE

But do you feel full inside your bones?

LAYLA

An emotion that I save for babies and kittens.

BLUES CHANTEUSE

I see a difficult choice that made my life so vital it was worth whatever it took.

LAYLA

I can see you made the vital choice. And Diahlo too. I just can't live beneath a certain standard. Even if I'm suffering inside. I can't. I'm comfort--corrupt.

BLUES CHANTEUSE

That's where a stay on the continent, Africa, would do you good.

LAYLA

I've taken trips there. I've even taken students on trips there.

BLUES CHANTEUSE

I said a stay. Get out of the hotel. Live there, eat with the people, and see how they have cohesive society without all our creature comforts.

LAYLA

(Picks up her bags and rises to go) The Blues Chanteuse. Love the name. I've gotta get back to the conference. It's been enlightening.

(Walks away as BLUES CHANTEUSE plays softly as if Layla had never been there. Layla walks back,)

LAYLA

I've attended conferences for years now. It seems it's a pressure cooker for somebody to go apeshit crazy. I roomed with a woman who had a nervous breakdown. Ambulance, stretcher, hospital, the whole bit. I saw a marriage fall completely apart. The couple divorced after it. I'm very sane. I can't prove my worth any more than what I'm doing. And I will not commit financial suicide.

[Layla sets her shoulders straight, walks off)

END SCENE

SCENE SIX

[Outside the convention center, it's windy. Layla primps. Her outfits get ever more precious; Diahlo is sitting down, looking winded]

LAYLA

You need a personal assistant.

DIAHLO
I have a wife. I need a smoke.
[Layla gives him an electronic cigarette]
LAYLA
Healthier for you…and me.
DIAHLO
The slaughter of the lamb.
LAYLA
Diahlo, outdated. I'm pulling you kicking and screaming into the river that's passing by right now.
DIAHLO
To drown with you?
LAYLA
You lose credence when you refuse to update.
DIAHLO
We call that co--opted.
LAYLA
Outdated concept.
DIAHLO
I pledge allegiance to the flag.
[Two professors come a few feet away]
DR. KWAME MONTAGUE
Better get a pic.
CHIZ
He's on his last leg.
DR. KWAME MONTAGUE
That's cold, man. We gon get there someday.
CHIZ
Nah. They invented the Dorian Gray cocktail. Stay young, fall apart at the end, and die ugly as sin.

[They take pics while Layla talk and Diahlo smokes.
Diahlo walks away with difficulty.
Layla watches him, then walks over and joins the two Profs]

DR. KWAME MONTAGUE

His mistake: refusing to kiss ass or knock boots. Hold that militant shit until after you make tenure. Any fool knows that.

[They slap hands]

LAYLA

Those guys. They tackled the Moby Dicks of academia. That was his job. Their job. Pave the way.

CHIZ

Somebody did it for him. And got no glory. He complains too much.

LAYLA

You know…you don't have to outgay the gay thing with me. I get it already.

CHIZ

No, I fit the stereotype. I have since forever. When I was a baby, I was "put my hand on my hip and let my backbone slip, I do the hokey-- pokey, and I turn it all around. That's what it's all about."

LAYLA

Yeah, but--

CHIZ

Yeah, but nothing. I'm pretending when I don't flaunt it.

LAYLA

You're just RuPaul under the skin?

CHIZ

Under, over, all around. There should be a place for everyone in this world, not just in San Francisco. LGBT is the same tossed salad as the rest of the world.

LAYLA

We, meaning smart blacks, polite blacks, were trained to march into society like toy soldiers

(The two began marching, but he has fun while Layla becomes distraught)

CHIZ

Little toy soldiers

LAYLA

I never bought Cliff Huxtable's smiley face obstetrician. Growing up, I saw firsthand stressed out professionals, like Toni Morrison's doctor in *Song of Solomon,* wound up, overworked and marching into society as beautiful as black--and--white TV.

CHIZ

In the sixties Baraka said, "The only good thing about TV is that colored people aren't on it."
[Engages in mimicry of TV character George Jefferson]
Don't you get tired of the facade?
[He imitates Redd Foxx]
Don't you get tired of the façade?
[He imitates Louise Jefferson and George Jefferson]
I know they got tired of the façade.
[He sings the Fresh Prince of Bel Air theme song]
Tired yet of the façade?

LAYLA

Been tired.

CHIZ

Then let it go.

LAYLA

[Lets out a loud African vocal riff and dances]
I will.

CHIZ

[Joins her]
Not you will. You do it. You are it. You. You. Nobody but you.

END SCENE

SCENE SEVEN

[Gunshots, rapid machinegun fire plays over and over. The Last Brother with a luggage carrier that's partially open, Layla and Chiz walk out of the convention proper into the foyer. There is a great commotion behind them.]

LAYLA

Why would you bring a gun, a weapon, into this venue? Are you trying to get us all kicked out of here?

[The shots keep echoing. It becomes clear it's a tape. The Last Professor shuts off the tape remotely with a handheld device]

THE LAST BROTHER

It's an academic/performance piece. The Gun as the Ultimate Performance Poem. George Zimmerman killed Trayvon Martin, got acquitted for it, and switched from security guard to painter, boxer, whatever he wants. One round, point blank to the chest. The Gun is the steel metaphor to dominate and lay waste. Even Hollywood uses the Gun s the United States' international calling card.

LAYLA

Is it loaded?

THE LAST BROTHER

Of course not. We aren't the Black Panthers in Sacramento, 1966, legally carrying loaded weapons in broad daylight. The man changes the law as soon as colored folk use it as a weapon.

[Chiz pulls out an ambulance siren from the Last Brother's case. It begins blinking. A sound emits, like a siren, but the Last Brother shuts it off immediately.]

CHIZ

Dayyum! Shazam!

LAYLA

And what is that supposed to represent?

THE LAST BROTHER

In its wake The Gun leaves only smoke and powder. The ambulance picks up the pieces.

[He pulls out a string of what looks at first like paper dolls, but what are paper panthers. Chiz gives one end of them to Layla and holds the other end. It stretches across the stage.]

CHIZ

What the eff? Bro, you're a magician.

THE LAST BROTHER

The Gun shattered the boundary between the personal and the political. The Panthers labeled the black intellectuals "paper panthers."

CHIZ

Are you saying that all of us here are nothing but paper dolls twisting in the winds of academia?

THE LAST BROTHER

The Oxford intellectuals in the 1920s and 1930s fighting Fascism called it "detached intelligence" -- a stance that had to be sacrificed to defeat Fascism.

LAYLA

You could have made all these points without bringing a gun into the room.

[She and the Chiz begin folding paper panther dolls back into one.]

THE LAST BROTHER

No, I couldn't have. All these points have been made and argued since Nat Turner. This split between conscience and activism is not new.

LAYLA

But our positions in the academy are new. If we get booted out of the academy, we have nowhere to go. [Layla holds the paper panthers to her bosom]

THE LAST BROTHER

Nowhere but home. The split between the two groups of black militants shattered the viability of "detached intelligence" in the San Francisco Bay Area. The BPP cut through the pacifistic and rhetorical gestures and stance of the cultural nationalists with the pragmatism of the bullet. It resolved the issue of activism.

CHIZ

How active should an activist be?

THE LAST BROTHER

Ready to die for the cause. You know what Harriet Tubman told her charges who wanted to return to the plantation once they'd gone underground?

LAYLA

If you turn back, I'll shoot you. There isn't going to be any shooting here, but we're not turning back. [With that resolve, she places the paper panthers back into the case.]

We are not marching out of the academy just because it's plagued with racism.

CHIZ

And sexism. And homophobia. And ageism. And elitism.

THE LAST BROTHER

So, Miss Layla, can I have your permission to put on this performance?

LAYLA

I'll make you a deal. You give the seminar attendees an oral précis of your performance before you begin, that's one. And, two, choose either the gun noise or the siren, not both.

THE LAST BROTHER

Afraid I'll drive somebody crazy?

LAYLA

Yes, quite frankly. I've seen it happen before.

THE LAST BROTHER

Deal.

END SCENE

SCENE EIGHT

LAYLA

Remember when Alice Walker told feminists to only have one child?

DIAHLO

Nope. I was busy making babies and building houses.

LAYLA

How many?

DIAHLO

Children? Houses?

LAYLA

Children, Diahlo.

DIAHLO

Nine. that I claim. Always had my own agenda.

LAYLA

Is it true?

DIAHLO

What?

LAYLA

I can finally ask. Even if I don't get an answer. You guys made a pact in the East Village way before shit went down? Way before nationalism?

DIAHLO

What's the word?

LAYLA

I'm asking you. You the griot. Here's the pact: that all of you were going for critical success and marrying white women?

DIAHLO

Where'd you hear that nonsense?

LAYLA

Read it in somebody's memoir.

DIAHLO

The curse of the academic. Read too much.

LAYLA

True? Or falsehood?

DIAHLO

I seem to remember some such inconsequential bullshit.

LAYLA

Was it b.s. when you made babies behind it?

DIAHLO

I'm proud of all my offspring. Black, Brown, white.

LAYLA

Equal opportunity baby daddy.

DIAHLO

Slow down, sweetheart. Have you never been 21?

LAYLA

Those decisions led to a raft of other decisions, some of which impacted me directly.

DIAHLO

Dr. Ms. Professor, throw in that we were opening doors to a closed house. Forgive us if we mistook a haunted house for a mansion. It looked like one.

LAYLA

It wasn't!

DIAHLO

1960 was a time when a black boy from nowhere needed credentials. We had managed to get educated. What was our next step?

LAYLA

To step over sisters and get a white woman.

DIAHLO

Believe it or not, that was a very radical move then.

LAYLA

Not now. It’s sanctioned by society. That’s what it led to.

DIAHLO

I corrected my situation. Married a sister. Two as a matter of fact. You could say I overcorrected.

LAYLA

Obligatory love?

DIAHLO

What more do you want? That no one be historically illogical? The end of segregation had everyone fleeing to the land of unintended consequences.

LAYLA

Your acts were intentional.

DIAHLO

What do you want, Layla?

LAYLA

Just admit that your motives weren’t pure.

DIAHLO

[Laughs] Come feel my horns…I’m proud of you, Dr., you’re my child, [motions to conference sign]. I’m proud of these puffed--up Negroes, too -- my beneficiaries.

[Pulls out a folding cane and snaps it open]

LAYLA

I didn’t see that at the airport.

DIAHLO

You weren't looking for it.

END SCENE

LAST SCENE [NINE]

[At the airport terminal. It's daytime and busier.]

DIAHLO

[Talking to himself] Okay, Suze Orman. I'm putting my paper in order. Franklin, Lincoln, Jefferson, Washington. Face up, dead prezzes. [Puts his receipts in a neat pile] I only spent $136.

[Puts the money away, puts the receipts in his case, closes his eyes, taps his feet to the airport Muzak, a smile on his face. A prof with a carry--on walks up to Diahlo and taps him, startling him.]

DR. PRETTYMAN

Diahlo.

DIAHLO

Man, what, what, who died? [Relaxes when he sees it's a friend. They greet each other.] We've been at this for half a century? Every day seems like I get notice of a death.

DR. PRETTYMAN

Probably a brother. The women outlive us.

DIAHLO

No matter how much we dog them, eh?

DR. PRETTYMAN

Just makes em stronger.

DIAHLO

Man, what'd you pull out of this conference? The gist?

DR. PRETTYMAN

Oh man, I got lucky. That's why you didn't see me that much.

[He puts back on his wedding ring] Man, love that you don't dip. But I never had that one love.

DIAHLO

Maybe you had it and didn't recognize it. Too blind to see.

DR. PRETTYMAN

Nah, man, my eyes been open since day one. Wide open. I'm telling you, every time I get lucky, I know there's no such thing as fidelity.

DIAHLO

Lucky, humph. That's why.

DR. PRETTYMAN

Why what?

DIAHLO

You have to close your eyes and let the ideal of love carry you through.

DR. PRETTYMAN

Idea or ideal?

DIAHLO

Both. With love. It's with black studies too. Be true to the idea. Be true to the ideal.

[They do a brother--hug]

Go back through those women. Find the one. Apologize for your oversight. And, bro, you ain't got all day and all night.

[Dr. Prettyman bids him adieu. Diahlo sits down, thoroughly tired, and tries to rest but pops into action, pulls out wallet, starts counting his money and mumbling.]

Okay, Suze Lesbian. Am I right with you? Shit. I take good advice. I'm a good student.

(Stands as if he's giving a eulogy)

This man, this product of his time, space and mud, loved houses and buildings as much as he loved any person. That was his curse and his joy. Blueprints. Plans.

(Stumbles a bit and has to use his cane to steady himself) I stood for the cause. I built a discipline. Carter G. Woodson laid the foundation. I helped complete it. (sits)

His second wife -- the one between the first and fourth ones, they married twice -- she was the only one who got it, that he found a bay window as intriguing as a woman in the nude. Designing the rotunda for City Hall gave him as much pride of performance as producing any one of his four boys. Built that way. (gets his carry--on, hobbles offstage)

END PLAY

Questions for Discussion

1. Some terms for study: paradigm, promulgate, propensity, trope, antediluvian.
2. What is a chanteuse?
3. Who are Bricktop, Estelle Yancey, Victoria Spivey and Louis Armstrong? Listen to any one of these vocalists to get a flavor for what The Blues Chanteuse might sound like.
4. What is the real estate KKK?
5. Does Diahlo in Act One, Scene One have anxiety or arrogance?
6. Does Diahlo's use of what some would term vulgarity make him vulgar or racist or sexist? Why or why not?
7. How would you make this into a film?

essays

Five Comrades in The Black Panther Party, 1967--1970

Bobby Seale and Huey Newton came to San Francisco State in the spring of '67 to recruit at the same time Clorox, Kaiser and IBM came. The two men stood side by side, gave their spiel, their sign up sheets laid out in the back of the room. My roommates and I wore our hair natural and favored pea coats, hip ponchos and boots. But I hesitated when they signed to join the BPP, remembering my civil servant mother's warning about signing my name to radical causes.
While some came to call it the Summer of Love, for those of us in the belly of the beast--urban America, it was another long, hot summer. In August I joined.

We five young women became the first wave of students from San Francisco State to join the Black Panther Party. We were referred to as sisters with skills. Evelyn handled finances, Janice became Bobby Seale's scheduler, Betty managed the BPP office, and Jo Ann corralled the troops. I worked on the BPP Intercommunal Newspaper with Eldridge and Kathleen Cleaver.

Some of the first issues of the paper were laid out at The Black House. It's no coincidence that that stately Victorian on Broderick St. was a prime gathering spot for poetry readings, jazz sets and political talks; poets, dancers, musicians, students, party people and the lumpen mixed and mingled for a time at this home of Eldridge Cleaver and poet--playwright Marvin X. The Black House unity didn't last; the cultural nationalists, who advocated a black--only cultural milieu, and the militant Panthers, who welcomed alliances with radical whites, split.

The Panthers were creating a new language, what Jean--Paul Sartre calls superlanguage. Sartre calls it language distortion, a means by which the colonized deconstruct their oppression and reorder existence. Police became *pigs*; a deadly police raid became *a reign of terror*. We made the language, as Sartre identifies it, revolutionary and incantatory: *Off the pigs. Power to the people. All power to the people. Free Huey.*

Our gang of five affected policy and high--level decisions by virtue of our intense participation, outspokenness, our spacious Potomac St. flat which became a safe house, our connections to our families and communities in Oakland, Hunters' Point, the Sunset and Fillmore districts, and Iowa [shout out to Janice] where we grew up. Our parents and relatives provided money, housing, books, cars, meeting places, food and clothing to the party as documented by the FBI.

We also formed liaisons and romantic relationships with brothers in the party. From the upper echelon to the lumpen proletariat, we lived, slept, ate and cooked with the BPP, running up and down the state and the country, all of which was a natural development that resulted in many discussions on Potomac St. about the differences [and similarities] between brothers from the street and brothers on campus. We were the initial link between the campus and the party. Three of us married "brothers in the struggle" who also happened to be educated brothers. This is significant because our connections and intimacy [which some labeled promiscuity] connected brothers from the party with brothers from SF State. The BSU brothers like to talk about supplying the BPP with guns and money, but *this bridge called my back* supplied the people's army with equal and greater provision.

When Huey was arrested and jailed in the shootout in November 1967, the paper overnight became an international organ, and the BPP an international sensation. To the world the party surfaced as the radical arm of the civil rights movement. At that point, my work stepped up with the paper. Donations poured into the office for the Free Huey movement. Police and FBI surveillance intensified. Six months later, the killing of Bobby Hutton and the shooting/jailing of Eldridge led to a meeting outside in Mosswood Park in Oakland, across the street from Kaiser Permanente Hospital. We met in the park because we didn't want the FBI to hear the tape from Huey. On it, he reorganized the party, and to my surprise, appointed me editor--in--chief during Eldridge's jail stay.

This changed all the dynamics. School became irrelevant. SF State had been indifferent and even hostile to Negro students for so long that the strongest sense of belonging had come from black sororities and fraternities. However, after going down South and participating in the Freedom Rides in the summer of 1966, a multiracial contingent of students returned to radicalize the campus. Those students developed the Tutorial Program at SF State into a community--based web of free after school tutoring centers in the Mission, Fillmore and Potrero Hill. This campus program was a first concrete radicalization for many. My roommates and I tutored and ran several of the centers.

Many idealistic students in the sixties dropped out and some devoted lives to the movement; by the time they returned to campus, many had changed their class affiliation. My friends and I dropped out and worked in the BPP full time. We eventually returned to campus too, armed, not only with actual weapons, but with a new consciousness about education, service, the poor, the police and the military, oppression, and civil and human rights. Our experience in the party helped us envision a viability in revitalizing and connecting to our community versus fleeing into the mainstream, corporate

America or the professions as a distanced, glancing downward teacher or social worker. No matter our background, and all five of us came from two--parent, middle--class families, we became aware of the class contradictions in the American dream.

I saw Bobby Seale recently and had to remind him who I was by recalling the roommates. He said, quite sincerely, “Which one was my girlfriend?” I wasn’t insulted. After all, he was looking back 40 years, and we were far more than girlfriends.

Questions for Discussion

1. How did the black power movement differ from the civil rights movement?
2. Why does the author include this essay about a political moment in a handbook about literary aesthetics?
3. To whom or what does this handbook pay homage?

Meeting LeRoi Jones

I transferred as a junior psychology major to San Francisco State in Spring, 1966. That semester, the Negro Student Association transformed into the nation's first Black Student Union. I liked it far more than the status-conscious Greeks and color-struck sororities and got involved pronto. The entire college turned radical when a group of students returned to campus from the Freedom Bus Rides in the South that summer (1966). I began tutoring at an inner city tutorial center and going to all kinds of arts and poetry events. As a poet, I fell in with the Black Arts Movement and fought for the student body funds to bring LeRoi Jones (later Amiri Baraka), Sonia Sanchez, Gwendolyn Brooks and Don L. Lee (later Haki Mathubuti) to campus. The cities were aflame, the nation was at war, and I was smack dab on the front line of revolution and resistance. As a black activist, I advocated for change in the black community in Oakland and San Francisco. The two factions split - the artists and the activists - and I had to choose, eventually becoming the editor-in-chief of the Black Panther Party newspaper.

I first saw LeRoi Jones in the flesh, at his vociferous best, at the student body funding debate. I was stone-ass surprised that he was even there. I mean I thought of him as a Big Important Writer from the East Coast in a Tweed Coat with Books under His Arm squirreled away from us except for class. I knew he was due to teach a class; I had even been assigned by the BSU prez to find him and his wife Sylvia (later to become Amina) an apartment at which task I failed after two weeks of walking up and down the hills of the Fillmore and the Haight with $250 in cash in my purse. They ended up having to stay at the Travel-lodge on Market St. until someone else, more on the ball, found them a pad; some other soul got them from the airport. Forever after when I passed Travel-Lodge situated on the street leading to the Bay Bridge I felt mortification at failing the test. And here he was, not in his book-lined study, not surrounded by Balzac, Genet, Ionesco, or Brecht, not hunched over a Smith-Corona portable as inspiration poured from his fingertips, not on the phone long distance with some big bubba tubba negotiating another run of "Dutchman." Nope, he had left beat nihilism for black nationalism, He was with us, giving much lip to the punk-ass white boys who controlled the student body budget and wanted, for some perverse reason that I'm sure would never have occurred to them in their native Stanislaus or Siskiyou counties to pick a fight with the BSU over our altogether legitimate and defensible hiring of LeRoi. We packed the classroom for the meeting with students - black, white, Hispanic, Asian - and community people, all black and formidable. Academia's cherubs, goodbye. We drowned them, washed over them in a wave of derision. Every time they tried business as usual, we up-against-the-wall-motherfuckered them. The white boys got tired real quick of beating their heads against a united front and they grudgingly agreed to give it up. Yea-us. LeRoi immediately set the BSU to rehearsing and performing his play "Black Mass." We were the Black Arts and Culture Troupe, we got a van, we ran up costumes at the pad, we put on shows within a matter of days, I was the warm-up act, reading poetry, our prez wrote a play, "Night-time is the

Right Time," and we were gone, black train down the black track, LeRoi was the engine; we had an array of talent in the BSU, actors, singers, modern dancers, to supply motive force, the cars, if you will, and I, as usual, was the caboose. The prez, saying I was the quintessential naysayer, even gave me a part in the play, the last line which I delivered and even changed if I chose, since the clapping and the right-ons started just before it and nobody could hear me say squat. We took the show to colleges, centers and anyplace they'd let us in-East Palo Alto, West Oakland, Western Addition, South Berkeley, Marin City, Seaside, Hunter's Point.
The prez' play was big fun to perform. No Romeo and Juliet here; no boy-gets girl, boy loses girl, boy gets her back stuff here. We improvised a riot, more like man gets mad, man gets Molotov, woman throws it. The play, as written, was a one-page set of instructions like this:

PROLOGUE
A single light shines on a man off to the side mad, making a Molotov cocktail. Across the stage, dancers rise from the flour, reaching upward; lighting goes from shadowy to bright. A voice projects:

Night time is the right time
for riot, for love
for surprising the man

Evening is our spring
If all we got is one day
Then we only have one night
Not a winter night
lonely bleak
desolate
Spring in the night
Wake up
Bloom into blackness
brothers and sisters
Burst wide open
Be/come
be/come
Yeah come hard
and then come out
Come out
Into the streets
Dance in the streets (Play "Dancing
in the Streets")
in the streets
Fight in the streets
Run in the streets
Throw a Molotov cocktail
in the streets
Die in the streets
Live and Die in the streets
Bring this society
to its knees
in the streets
Bring LBJ to his texas
cracker barrel knees
in the streets
Bring all the traitors
in the ivory towers
into the streets
Move into the streets

Reclaim society
in the streets

Scene One
Fat mama and a sister carrying
sorrow like a ball and chain beg their
brethren not to throw his Molotov
cocktail.

Scene Two
A younger brother watches as he
throws it, the police came looking
for him, He hides, and the mother
deliberates on whether to turn her
son in.

Scene Three
The police get vicious and kill him.
The younger brother announces he's
going to join the army. The mother
approves until she finds out it's the
Black Militia.

Scene Four
The mother decides she has nothing
left to lose, she joins up too. A
neighbor comes as she's leaving and
says (my line):
"Some people join church, I see you
joined the world."

Sometimes I threw in my grandma's old favorite, "Don't let no man drag you down," changing it, if people could hear me, to "Don't let the man drag you down," or the old standby, "You can do bad by yourself." But the point of the naysayer, as LeRoi explained it to us in class, was to show that quality of self-doubt in blacks that would always accompany liberating actions, but which would be drowned out by the exulting of the people at the moment of liberation.

Once, driving back from a show, I stood in the back of the van towering over LeRoi; I held onto the rail and observed him. He had a nice funny cackle of a laugh; he was a little guy who hunched; even standing here in my head, he's hunched in his little finely embroidered dashiki. A compact man. A nice man. Even a gentle man. He bantered, for heavens' sake. I liked him and not at all in a sexual way. Thank goodness, he didn't give off that vibe. He was short, anyway. His vibe was let's get going, let's do business, let's put on a really good show. Onstage, on podium, he became the ferocious, shrill, harsh, demanding killer, scary.

The one time I saw him mix the two personas was his last night in town, our crowning performance at the Black House in the Fillmore district. The old Victorian that we all called the Black House was the portal to black fineness. LeRoi ranted, raved, screamed; he also talked soft and tender about his wife and the baby on the way. I got the shock of my life when he pointed her out. LeRoi Jones' wife! She had foreboding eyes and was taller than I was! I had to force myself not to gape. He married up not down! But I couldn't help staring. She was pregnant, nearly due. Her belly bloomed out so perfectly pregnant you could see her enlarged belly button sticking out through the African cotton like a pacifier. I felt bad I was the cause of her and the unborn child staying in a motel. Her hair surrounded her proudness like so many twisted branches of a tree. Even with the baby blooming, she retained a feminine slim curve to her dancer's figure. And she talked about California like it had a tail. She did not like California, San Francisco, the

Bay Area, and by extension, us. California niggahs are out to lunch, I heard her say loudly several times that night. She insisted on dancing a solo bit. My friends and I gave each other the elbows. So supple she looked boneless, she rolled over on her bloomy stomach as if it were a bag of raked leaves. When she finished her dance, she got up and went upstairs. I heard her say, These San Francisco bloods are trifling-ass. Zora Neale says language is like money. Well, Sylvia Jones paid us niggardly wage that night. Grandma's old rose-jumping, hide and seek rhyme came to mind:

honey in the bee ball
I can't see y'all
all ain't hid
caint hide over

There was no hiding from her. The applause at the end of "Night Time's the Right Time" was prolonged. While they were making thunder, I mimicked Sylvia Jones:

don't wanna struggle, don't wanna work,
don't wanna make real change
humph, California, humph
a place with a whole lotta people who wanna do nothing
white folk here cuz they made it
black folk, what's your excuse?

Of course, people saw my grumble-face but they heard only the last few words.

Questions for Discussion

1. Throughout this handbook, you've encountered several versions or manifestations of the writer Amiri Baraka: fictively, as the prototype for Diahlo Green, in recollection, as LeRoi Jones, and poetically, as in "(not) forgotten man." Also, the back cover photos give another view of this seminal figure. Are these versions contradictory? Why or why not?
2. Compare and contrast his persona as a mentor in "Meeting LeRoi Jones" and "Life is a Carousel."
3. What is the meaning of his many name changes in his lifetime? Research the names he used and create a timeline for when he began using each name, starting from birth. If you've changed your name, how did that impact your life?
4. This handbook blends four genres. How does each contribute to your understanding of the Black Arts Movement? What have you found in your additional research that brought up doubts or confirmed assumptions about the BAM?

Some additional resources for studying the Black Arts Movement:

• • Kalamu ya Salaam. "Historical Background of the Black Arts Movement (BAM). October Gallery. http://octobergallery.com/2012/04/25/black-arts-movement-bam/

• • The Black Arts Repertory Theatre/School Archived November 12, 1999, at the Wayback Machine.

• • Finkelman, Paul, ed. (2009). *Encyclopedia of African American History.* **1**. Oxford: Oxford University Press. p. 187. ISBN 9780195167795.

• • "A Brief Guide to the Black Arts Movement". poets.org. February 19, 2014.

• • Rojas, Fabio . *web.b.ebscohost.com.*

• • Cheryl Higashida, *Black Internationalist Feminism: Women Writers of the Black Left, 1945-1995*, University of Illinois Press, 2011, pp. 52–53.

• • Emmanuel S. Nelson, *The Greenwood Encyclopedia of Multiethnic American Literature: A — C*, Westport, CT: Greenwood Press, 2005, p. 387.

• • Smethurst, James E. *The Black Arts Movement: Nationalism in the 1960s and 1970s* (The John Hope Franklin Series in African American History and Culture). NC: The University of North Carolina Press, 2005.

• • Douglas, Robert L. *Resistance, Insurgence, and Identity: The Art of Mari Evans, Nelson Stevens, and the Black Arts Movement*. NJ: Africa World Press, 2008.

• • Bracey, John H. (2014). *SOS- Calling All Black People: A Black Arts Movement Reader.*

Massachusetts: University of Massachusetts Press. p. 18. *ISBN* 978-1-62534-031-3.

- • "A Gathering of the Tribes" (Place Matters, January 2012) includes biography of Steve Cannon. http://panopticonreview.blogspot.com/2015/03/in-celebration-of-50th-anniversary-of.html
- • Neal, Larry. "The Black Arts Movement". *A Turbulent Voyage: Readings in African American Studies*, ed. Floyd W. Hayes III. San Diego, California: Collegiate Press, 2000 (3rd edition). 236–246.
- • "Black Art". www.nathanielturner.com.
- • "Pop Music and the Spatialization of Race in the 1990s | The Gilder Lehrman Institute of American History". www.gilderlehrman.org. 2012-07-12..
- • "Amiri Baraka". Poetry Foundation. 2016-10-31.
- • Nielson, Erik. "White Surveillance of the Black Arts". web.b.ebscohost.com.
- • Peter, C.; Willick, D. (July 2, 2012). "Suzanne Jackson's Gallery 32 and Los Angeles's Burgeoning African American Arts Community". Nka Journal of Contemporary African Art. **2012** (30): 16–27. doi:10.1215/10757163-1496435.
- • "African and Asian Visual Artists Archive". VADS: the online resource for visual arts.
- • "In Celebration of the 50th Anniversary of the Black Arts Movement (BAM) And Its Ongoing Social, Cultural, and Aesthetic Legacies." The Panopticon Review. March 31, 2015

Praise for *Virgin Soul,* a novel by Judy Juanita (Viking, 2013)

"Funny and wise . . . a captivating tale about self-love told through the eyes of an unforgettable heroine."
—***Essence***

"Witty and deeply engaging . . . about ideas and the passions generated by revolution and romantic love."
—***Los Angeles Times***

"Electrifying . . . *Virgin Soul* yields an engaging coming-of-age story, one that recalls a turbulent era in captivating prose."
—***San Jose Mercury News***

"Juanita's prose immediately immerses the reader in the time and place of its lead character. . . [who] progresses from middle-class "good girl" to member of the Black Panthers, witnessing and experiencing the poverty, violence, excesses and rhetoric of the time, a transition handled by Juanita with assured matter-of-factness . . . The unique perspective she offers on a volatile period of American history gives the narrative immediacy and authenticity."
—***Publishers Weekly***

"An entertaining story of a young woman's experience with one of the most radical counterculture organizations in America 's history."
—***Bust Magazine***

“[With] rhythmic language and nervy dialog . . . this wild ride through the rise of the militant Black Panther Party highlights differing viewpoints within the civil rights movement of the Vietnam era. Fans of Bernice McFadden will enjoy discovering this new author.”
—***Library Journal***

“An intriguing look at coming-of-age in the 1960s.”
—***Booklist***

"*Virgin Soul* is first class awesome, every page a crackling hungry flame. This novel about a young studious woman immersed in the black revolutionary experience of 60's Berkeley has a freshness and bright ardor that is rare in this lazy climate of American fiction.”
—**Joy Williams**, author of ***State of Grace***

“Hard to believe it’s been almost fifty years since the formation of the Black Panthers. The novel captures that time’s particular combination of violence and possibility, and the urgency of young people who invested everything in the possibility of change, even as grand rhetoric was undercut by very human failings. Geniece is smart, wounded, hopeful, and tough. It's a pleasure to grow with her through these pages.”
—**Jean Thompson**, author of ***The Humanity Project*** and ***The Year We Left Home***

“*Virgin Soul* is Judy Juanita’s exciting debut, a coming-of-age novel set in a time of peace, love and revolution. Juanita presents a heroine, wise, naive and world-wary at eighteen who finds her voice in the Black Panthers’ deadly struggle for liberation in

1960s America . Though a work of historical fiction, ***Virgin Soul*** **is an intimate work, heart-breaking and compulsively readable.**"
—Evan Wright, author of *Generation Kill*

"A novel so unlike any I've read in years—a little of Al Young's poetry and humor, a little of Toni Cade Bambara's boldness, but Judy Juanita has given us a Bay Area in her own inimitable voice, which is California like no one else. She lays it out for you. With this writer, there is no half-steppin'."
—**Susan Straight**, author of ***Between Heaven and Here***

"Intense, riveting, spellbinding, this tour de force places the reader on the frontlines of the 1960's counter culture and the Black Power movement, one of the most turbulent times in American history. More than a coming of age novel, *Virgin Soul* is ultimately a meditation on love. It's about the love of Geniece's biological family and the family of radicals who adopt her. A must read."
—**Robert Alexander**, author of ***Servant of the People***

"Judy Juanita gives readers a very real look at that exciting and turbulent time through the eyes of her strong, questing protagonist. There are pages when the prose lifts into lyricism, so it should be no surprise that the author's writing has for years encompassed poetry as well as reporting. This is her first novel. I'm glad she wrote it and hope it won't be her last."
—**P.J. Grath**, bookseller, **Dog Ears Books**

ABOUT THE AUTHOR

Novelist, essayist, poet and playwright Judy Juanita's writing focuses on black culture and community, the Black Arts Movement, the Bay Area, its vigor and on the uniqueness of its politics, culture and art.

Her novel, *Virgin Soul*, was published hardcover by Viking, 2013, and in paperback by EquiDistance, 2017; its protagonist joins, as she did, the Black Panther Party in the sixties in the San Francisco Bay Area.

Her poetry has appeared in *13th Moon, Painted Bride Quarterly, Crab Orchard Review, Croton Review* and *Obsidian* Her plays have been produced in Oakland, San Francisco, Berkeley, LA, Winston-Salem and NYC.

Her collection of essays, *De Facto Feminism: Essays Straight Outta Oakland* (EquiDistance, 2016) looks at the gap between black and female empowerment. She resides in Oakland.

Picture by Kingmond Young

ABOUT THE AUTHOR

www.ingramcontent.com/pod-product-compliance
Lightning Source LLC
Chambersburg PA
CBHW071539100726
47908CB00004B/1441

* 9 7 8 0 9 7 1 6 3 5 2 2 7 *